# as it really was

Marilyn

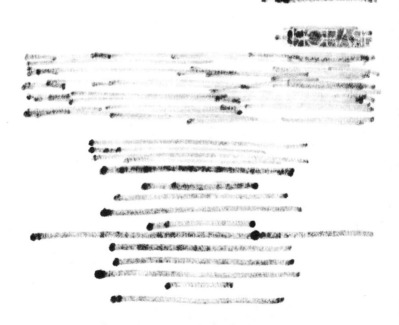

Printed in Victoria, BC, Canada

Note for Librarians: a cataloguing record for this book that includes Dewey Decimal Classification and US Library of Congress numbers is available from the Library and Archives of Canada. The complete cataloguing record can be obtained from their online database at:
www.collectionscanada.ca/amicus/index-e.html

TRAFFORD

This book was published on-demand in cooperation with Trafford Publishing. On-demand publishing is a unique process and service of making a book available for retail sales to the public taking advantage of on-demand manufacturing and Internet marketing. On-demand publishing includes promotions, retail sales, manufacturing, order fulfilment, accounting and collecting royalties on behalf of the author.

Offices in Canada, USA, UK, Ireland and Spain.

book sales for North America and international:

Trafford Publishing, 6E–2333 Government St.,
Victoria, BC V8T 4P4 CANADA
phone 250 383 6864    toll-free 1 888 232 4444
fax 250 383 6804    email to orders@trafford.com

book sales in Europe:

Trafford Publishing (UK) Ltd., Enterprise House, Wistaston Road Business Centre,
Crewe, Cheshire CW2 7RP UNITED KINGDOM
phone 01270 251 396    local rate 0845 230 9601
facsimile 01270 254 983    orders.uk@trafford.com

order online at:
www.trafford.com/robots/04-0481.html

10    9    8    7    6    5    4    3    2    1

# Introduction

Adam and Eve were created but were not the first man and woman on earth in any understanding - even symbolic. Life started much as Darwin worked out. When Adam and Eve were expelled from Eden there were evolved humans already living on the earth. Cain went to Nod after murdering Able and found a woman he made his wife and with whom he had at least one child, Genesis, chapter 4, verses 16 and 17. Then in Genesis, chapter 6, "sons of God" found "daughters of men" they were attracted to, and took them for wives.

Who other than male descendants from Adam and Eve were the "sons of God", and who else were the "daughters of men", but the daughters of evolved human beings? Christian theology has maintained that the "sons of God" were angels – although angels are supposed to be asexual or sexless according to religion. Also, God, when given a gender, has, according to Christianity conceived only one child, His only begotten Son, Jesus Christ. The other monotheistic faiths do not believe God "conceived" any children.

With an open mind it makes sense that Adam and Eve were not the first man and woman on earth, even according to the Bible. This does not deny what the Bible states but gives a new understanding to what has been *taught* from it.

This new understanding does not contradict what science has discovered either.

Who were Adam and Eve and why are they so important? Why were they created?

Who or what is God?

Why did the Jewish people stoically maintain that there was one God and that they were the chosen race?

Adam and Eve were created in human form because the most developed, evolved life on earth was in that form. Mankind was not made in the image of God - that would have been elevating man and debasing God. Mankind was made by God's representatives because God wanted mankind to know Him. God has had representatives on earth in the form of prophets, angels or inspired people throughout history.

God the Creator wanted to impart spiritual truths to the evolved world. As a result He embodied "spiritual" energy in human form. These "Gods", because Genesis does use and refer to the plural when speaking about the makers of mankind, made Adam and Eve (men and women) in the image of themselves. (Genesis, chapter 1 verses 26 and 27) They were to teach Adam and Eve about how the world was created and about there being one God, the Creator of all. Obviously this was done in a simple way, but it is basically scientifically correct.   It was to be developed later in the earth's history, in God's time

Who or what is God?   God is the creative life force or energy of the universe which was humanised through the Jewish faith.   This was perpetuated by Christianity.   Energy is the foundation of creation. Just because God can not be proved to be an old man with long robes and flowing grey hair and beard does not mean He does not exist in some form.   God "is" and as He said to Moses through the burning bush "I am that I am".

How could God the Father, the Creator of the universe, have been confined to an earthly body?

We humans inhabit one microscopic part of one universe in the cosmos. By the standards of the cosmos our bodies are "puny", yet they are wonderful and made up of billions of cells. To the microbes that live on each body, if they had the comprehension, each cell is like a planet and each organ or limb a galaxy.   Each body is a universe to those microbes on it.   In a similar way, but on a gigantic scale, "God" is the cosmos and his "body" is made up of all the planets and stars. This is not so different from the concept of the microcosm and macrocosm of the Middle Ages.   And as abuses heaped on human bodies take their toll, so the earth suffers under the excesses and imbalances heaped on it.   All this links with the Gaia theory.

There is a force of evil. It is pure destruction and cannot create. It is the antithesis of God and is commonly known as Satan or the Devil, but in reality, it is a power much stronger.

The Jewish people stoically maintained a belief in one God and had a special task to do. They considered themselves the "chosen race" because of their special relationship with "God". Jesus was born a Jew because the Jews believed in "God" and were monotheistic. The purpose of Jesus' life was to try and purify / simplify Judaism, to deflect the growth and popularity of the Pharisaical sect which overburdened the Jewish people with laws which made the practice of their religion complicated, and detracted from the crux of spirituality, God. Because the Jews as a nation did not listen to Him, a new religion was founded and became known as Christianity.

Apart from the Copernicus / Galileo belief that the sun was the centre of our universe, and Darwin's theory of evolution, there has not been a greater challenge to traditional scripture. Until our modern time there could not have been this challenge to the traditional scriptural rendering of our history. Now, with scientific facts, the church is stymied. It is possible to rectify this. I start with this book, the first of a new series.

It is possible to unite scientific and religious understanding. It starts with the Creation story itself.

# CONTENTS

## As It Really Was

Many thousands of years ago mankind revered the power of nature.  Not having any understanding of how nature worked, but knowing how totally dependent it was on nature, mankind understood that it contained superior power.  For this reason natural happenings were seen as phenomena and sometimes miracles.  With respect and fear, or maybe fear and respect, aspects of nature were worshipped.  Religion was born and people who specialised in interpreting natural signs as omens and portents were the first priests and priestesses. They wielded enormous power because mankind knew that their lives depended on a beneficent nature for survival.  Sacrifices, certain behaviours and even bodily mutilation were demanded, depending on circumstance.  Astronomy was devised as an aid to understanding nature.

It must have been "Adam and Eve" who passed on the Creation Story known to the monotheistic religions.  Until the latter half of the nineteenth century the majority of Westerners believed it without question.  It is a simplistic explanation of the creation of our universe, our world and the origins of mankind.  There are still people of faith who can accept it.  Science has shown that the order of creation is broadly correct although it is questionable how days and nights could exist before the sun and moon were created.  In Genesis chapter 1 verse 3,

*"God said, Let there be light: and there was light."*
Following immediately verse 4 states,

*"And God saw the light, that it was good: and God divided the light from the darkness."*
Verse 5 continues,

*"And God called the light Day and the darkness he called Night.   And the evening and the morning were the first day."*

However on the fourth day of creation according to the Bible, Genesis chapter 1 verses 14 – 18, states,

*"And God said, Let there be lights in the firmament of heaven to divide the day from the night; and let them be for signs, and for seasons, and for days and years: And let them be for lights in the firmament of heaven to give light upon the earth: and it was so.   And God made two great lights; the greater light to rule the day, and the lesser light to rule the night: he made the stars also.   And God set them in the firmament of heaven to give light upon the earth, And to rule over the day and over the night, and to divide the light from the darkness: and God saw that it was good."*

Additionally, we are told that each act of creation took a day and although this has been taken literally, the Bible also states that a day is a thousand years to the Lord.   (Psalm 90 verse 4 and 2 Peter chapter 3 verse 8)   However, science shows that even a thousand years was not enough, so some take the timing as figurative. Even with the above discrepancies either accepted or compromised over by people of faith, fossils and dinosaurs and primitive human life are not accounted for.

Scientists state that our world was made out of gases produced from a white hole. A white hole is the opposite of a black hole. While a black hole sucks into itself all that is in its way a white hole emits matter. A white hole is an inverted black hole. When a black hole is full it turns inside out and ejects "elements" which cannot be further decomposed. These elements are the building blocks of life and have been re-created from the "compounds" drawn into the black hole and burnt in the intense fire of its interior. Chemically all is new. When a white hole pours out refined elements, that part of the universe starts creating anew and atomic energy is in the atmosphere.

The basis of the universe is energy. Every cell of every thing in the universe contains it and is capable of emitting it directly or indirectly. Equally, when good or evil are created either by thoughts, words, or deeds corresponding energy is sent out into the universe. This is done through vibrations which are another form of energy. While every galaxy has a black hole, I believe it is the combined evil energy within each galaxy that forms itself into the black hole. When the black hole is eventually full and there is no set time frame for this, it inverts to become a white hole and new matter is emitted after having been through intense fire which purifies it making it chemically new and capable of creating new life. This is the real "hell fire" where evil is destroyed. From it the light is separated from the darkness as stated in Genesis chapter 1 verses 3 and 4.

*"God said, Let there be light: and there was light. And God saw the light, that it was good: and God divided the light from the darkness."*

On the first day of creation, the light that separated from the darkness and which pleased God was the recreation of elements that could create our world. These are the elements that were ejected from the white hole, refined and purified after burning in the intense fire of the interior of the black hole which preceded it. After destruction there was creation.

The story recorded in Holy Scripture that all humankind is descended from Adam and Eve is also questioned by scientific data. Although some believe the Bible implicitly, over and above scientific statements, science is confident that it has proved mankind was on the earth long before Adam and Eve were created. Those who accept this understand the story of Adam and Eve as symbolic in some way. However, there are clues in the Bible that Adam and Eve were not the first man and woman on earth even though they were specially created. In chapter 6 verses 1 and 2 of Genesis is the following,

*"And it came to pass, when men began to multiply on the face of the earth, and daughters were born unto them, That the sons of God saw the daughters of men that they were fair; and they took them wives of all which they chose."*

Surely this shows that male descendants of Adam and Eve *("the sons of God")* chose to marry women who were children of evolved humans *("daughters of men")*. The traditional understanding of *"the sons of God"* has been, and still is, angels.

After Adam and Eve had been expelled from Eden they had two sons, Cain and Abel. Jealousy caused Cain to murder Abel. In fear of his life and with a very guilty conscience, Cain left his parents and journeyed to a place called Nod where he found a woman he wanted to make his wife! (Genesis chapter 4 verses 16 and 17) Where had the people of Nod come from when we are told only of Adam, Eve and their two sons at this point?

Darwin and Science were right that mankind evolved, though Darwin has been badly misrepresented by people who believe what he wrote meant that humans were directly descended from apes. This is probably a result of the famous debate about the origins of man between the Church and Science in 1860. Darwin stood for scientific understanding and was represented by

T.H. Huxley, a close friend and supporter. Samuel Wilberforce, a popular theologian as well as the Bishop of Oxford, represented the Church. Neither side won: the Church was discredited and Darwin lampooned. Darwin's belief was that humans and primates shared a common ancestor in the far past and that then, for certain reasons, the progressive development of each diverged. This is not an uncommon natural phenomenon. In the case of humans, we are genetically 98.5 per cent similar to primates. However, the 1.5 per cent shows that a small percentage represents some significant differences.

According to more recent research American scientists state that chimpanzees, one branch of the primate family, are 99.4 per cent similar to humans. It is therefore credible that in the far distant past humans did share a common ancestor with primates.

## What is Good and Evil?

Good and evil are ways of understanding right and wrong. To live within a social structure rules or laws are necessary to make living in such a way tenable for everyone. Long before the Ten Commandments were given to the Israelites by Moses, the civilisations of Egypt, Mesopotamia and Phoenicia as well as Greece and the Aegean, were established and had laws. Hammurabi, King of Babylon, wrote a still famous code of law a few hundred years before Moses was born. Hammurabi developed the laws and writing system that had already been established in Mesopotamia. The Ten Commandments brought down from Mount Sinai by Moses became the basis of Jewish law and, much later through Christianity, large areas of the world.

The Ten Commandments were given as a guide to living. The only penalty attached to them when brought down from Mount Sinai by Moses was that if the Hebrews failed to acknowledge and worship God as the only god, **they, the Hebrews**, would suffer as would each of **their** subsequent generations up to the third or fourth. (Exodus chapter 20 verses 3 – 5) The penalties for breaking the remaining commandments were devised by man later. It is obvious if you kill, steal or want what is not yours you will cause suffering and problems to the members of your community who have been wronged. There are likely to be disputes and retribution. For these reasons,

punishments  were meted out to those who broke
the commandments as a deterrent to others.

What really are good and evil?    Being good is
**always trying** to treat other people as you would
like to be treated and being evil is **deliberately**
harming others in some way.    Sinning covers
those actions that religion, supported by society,
does not want its members to do.    Laws were
frequently created with the support of religion and
had the power of fear attached to breaking them.
These include dressing in certain ways, eating or
refraining from specific foods and observing
unquestioningly certain rituals.    Generally they
were devised in the belief they were beneficial to
the community as a whole.

## Denying God

Denying God does not stop him existing if he is
real.  Those who do believe claim he is the creator
of the universe and everything in it.   They also
claim he sees everything, knows everything and is
everywhere.  Many also believe that he came down
to earth as a baby boy called Jesus then grew into a
man and gave extraordinary teaching and healing
before being crucified on a cross.   It is also
believed by many that Jesus existed with God
before the Earth was created, coming to Earth to
do a special job, fulfilling God's command.   In the
prayer Jesus is quoted as saying on the night of
His betrayal, just before He was betrayed, written
in St John chapter 17 is the following,

" - - *I have finished the work which thou gavest
me to do.   And now, O Father, glorify me with
thine own self with the glory which I had with
thee before the world was.*"  (verses 4 and 5)

and

"- - *for thou lovedst me before the foundation of
the world.*"   (verse 23)

There are those who claim Jesus was God come
down to earth but there are also many who,
although they accept that Jesus lived on earth,
believe He had no divine status.

If there is a God who created the universe and sees all, knows all and is everywhere, how could such a great and powerful being be confined in one human body on one planet in one solar system of the whole universe, and still be God?    Even the most intelligent human beings alive today are not capable of creating life from nothing, let alone a universe from nothing.  So if the most intelligent people on earth today are inferior in ability to God, how could this God be the template for human beings?    Additionally, if as according to Holy Scripture and priests, we are all descended from Adam   and   Eve   who   sinned,   and   whose descendants   with   few   exceptions,   sinned progressively more, how could we truly be in God's image?  God is supposed to be perfect.

According to theological redactors and exegesis, in what is called the Creation Story written in Genesis chapter 1 and chapter 2, there are two versions of the same story.   They are placed one after the other.   Chapter 1 is a version supposed to post-date that of chapter 2.    It was after generations of passing on the Creation story orally these two renderings were written down like that because it seemed that the second amplified the first.   It is not known how many versions of the original Creation Story there were before Genesis was written down but it is accepted that there were numerous official interpreters of the biblical stories and that their explanations were not only official but accepted as authoritative.  Interpreters of Scripture were important people in biblical society and their prominence increased after the Babylonian exile. In time, probably by the third or second century B.C.E. both the text and the traditional understandings became intertwined and then canonised by Judaism and subsequently Christianity.   Interpreters still work at the texts but cannot change the text because since canonisation, they are considered to be genuine as they stand, and divinely inspired.

Both versions of the Creation Story not only state that God did the creating but also uses the plural "us" and "we" when describing those who did the creating of Adam and Eve.   It has been accepted that "God" was quoted as using the "royal we".  I question that.   So who were the others?   It is all the more challenging when the Bible states that God says,
"**Let us** *make man* **in our image, after our likeness**".   I do not believe that this was written using the "royal we".

I suggest that while "man", who is understood as "Adam and Eve", was made in the image of those who made man, those who made man, were God's *representatives* on earth.   God made these representatives in human form because that was the form of the most evolved creatures on earth. 4000 B.C.E. (Before the Common Era – before Jesus was born) was the time frame of the first civilisations evolving in Mesopotamia.   That means the first towns and cities were being built. Mankind had already evolved.   It was about 4000

B.C.E. that mankind became sophisticated enough to build and live in urban communities.   It was also the generally accepted time frame theologians accepted for the creation of Adam and Eve. Although there were several attempts to calculate the creation of Adam and Eve, it was Archbishop Usher (1581 – 1656), from Ireland, whose computations were widely accepted.      He concluded from his study of the Bible and discussions with respected Jewish scholars, that the Creation took place in 4004 B.C.E.   It is only very recently that some of the Church has considered Adam and Eve a generic representation of humankind as a whole, and the Creation Story a simple explanation of how life began on earth. These people also usually equate the biblical version of creation with other near middle-eastern creation stories like *"Enuma Elish"* and *"The Epic of Gilgamesh"*.

## God the Creator

There is a life force behind all of creation.    It
works on the cellular level and is in everything as
"electricity".      Every atom of everything that is
claimed in the Bible to have been created by God
contains this life force or electrical energy and it is
evidence of a power of creation.    The power of
creation called "God" by religion could be called
something  else  and  still  be  the  same  creative
power.    However the word "God" is familiar to
almost everyone  whether they  believe  in  his
existence or not.   Science uses different names for
fundamentally the same creative process.   Names
and  theories  are  invented  to  describe  what  is
discovered.     What is discovered are aspects or
details of the working of God the Creator.

*"What's in a name?   That which we call a rose*
*By any other name would smell as sweet."*

Shakespeare, "Romeo and Juliet", Act II, Scene ii,
Line 43

By means of this life force "God" is omnipresent,
omniscient and omnipotent as claimed by religion.
In other words, God is everywhere, present in
everything and knows everything because He is in
every cell of life.   By this means "it" the life force
or "He", God, is able to know  all  and  have
unlimited and ultimate power.  If cells are meant
to unite and create, as in producing new life, it will
happen.       This  is  not  confined  to  physical

reproduction as in plants and creatures. Mentally, new ideas are created and spiritually new understandings are found. Scientifically, some cells of matter will successfully unite and some will not whether by natural or manipulated means. The cells from any medium, solid, liquid or gaseous (gaseous includes any medium invisible to the human eye) can do this. However, within each cell is the potential for good or for bad, scientifically expressed as positive or negative. If the bad or negative predominates, potential harm results.

In the Garden of Eden were representatives from God. They were in human form because humans were the most highly evolved life form on earth. Their purpose was to create some men and women with spiritual potential, spiritual knowledge and above all an understanding of what life was really about. This meant explaining simply to them how the world and universe were created and that there was one God who was the Creator of everything.

I suggest that Eden existed on the Earth. It was an area chosen because the weather was ideal and there was an abundance of natural food. It was also secluded from tribes and communities of humans already living on the earth. The person in charge of this project on behalf of God was the person we know of later as Jesus.

Paul states in his Epistle to the Colossians, chapter 1 verse 16,

*"For by him* (referring to Jesus) *all things were created, that are in heaven, and that are in earth, visible and invisible - - all things were created by him, and for him."*

He is the one referred to as "God" in Genesis. "We" and "us" refer to Jesus and those who helped him create men and women.

"Adam" is a Hebrew word and as it is used in Genesis it is plural for mankind. It is also the root of the word for "earth" or "dust" in Hebrew. Evolved mankind came from the elements of the earth. Adam or the men were created biologically by a form of genetic engineering from the elements of the earth so they were similar to evolved mankind. Eve meaning "life" were women cloned from the men by using cells from the men's ribs. The created humans were then "blessed" so they could reproduce as evolved humans do. The reproductive capability of genetically engineered creatures and plants is not automatic. Such creatures and plants are sterile unless made with the ability to reproduce. God wanted the descendants of these people from Eden to "replenish" the earth. Genesis chapter 1 verse 28. In other words, those specially created were to replace those already on the earth. This shows that initially they had to be fertile, and subsequently there must have been people on the earth to be replaced. This is another indication that Adam and Eve were not the first people on earth. If no one was on the earth there was no one to replace. God did not want killing but intermarriage with evolved humans. This occurred and the creation story was passed on with a belief in the One God. The statement to be fruitful and multiply in Genesis chapter 1 verse 28 was a blessing on those that were created to be able to have children just as the evolved humans could. It was not an order from God, as interpreted by subsequent generations, to have as many children as possible, irrespective of the health of the mother and the family's ability to care properly for their children. Orthodox Jews and practising Roman Catholics still do not officially practice birth control under any circumstances. God's purpose to "replenish the earth" was to increase true spirituality on earth. People are still working towards that. It is not achieved by the number of children born but rather by the calibre of life those children lead when grown up.

## He in Us and We in Him

If God the Creator is the life force or energy that is in every cell of every thing it is a somewhat similar principle to the circulatory and nervous systems in our bodies.     By their circulatory systems humankind nourishes (keeps alive) their bodies and by their nervous systems humankind is aware of every part of their bodies.   "God", or this life force, provides life and is in every part of His creation.   Jesus is stated as saying in Matthew chapter 10 verse 29 that even a sparrow cannot fall without God knowing.   All life contains "God". This is how we really are in Him and He in us.

This life force or electrical energy is also how people can communicate with God and how He can communicate with people.   True prayer, meditation and inspiration are methods of such contact.   Also telepathy, clairvoyance and clairaudience are genuine methods of communication.   Humans are chemically about 2/3 water so make very good conductors of electricity and therefore have the potential to communicate in such ways effectively. Communications are not restricted to contact between humans and God, they can be made between people, or people and creatures, or even with evil.   Intuition works in a somewhat similar way.

St John chapter 15 explains this concept in a simple metaphor.   Jesus says he is the vine and his Father the "husbandman," that is, God is the gardener or farmer tending the vine, the one in ultimate control. Verses 4 – 6 explain more.

*"Abide in me and I you.   As the branch cannot bear fruit of itself, except it abide in the vine - - -*
*I am the vine, ye are the branches: He that abideth in me, and I in him, the same bringeth forth much fruit (i.e. spiritual understanding and treating others well, as you would want to be treated yourself) - - -*
*If a man abideth not in me, he is cast forth as a branch, and is withered and men gather them and cast them into the fire. - - -"*

Additionally, Jesus when praying to God on his last night on earth states according to St John in Chapter 17 verses 21 - 23, referring to his disciples and all who listen to them,

*"That they may be one; as thou Father, art in me, and I in thee, that they may be one in us: that the world may believe that thou hast sent me.*
*And the glory which thou gavest me I have given them; that they may be one, even as we are one:*
*I in them and thou in me - -."*

## The Soul and Spiritual Healing

I put forward that not only does the soul exist but it is the life force within us in every cell of our bodies and scientifically it is known as part of the DNA molecule. Within the DNA molecule are two strands of bases "woven" together to form a double helix. One of the strands is the template strand or sense strand containing the genetic code for any gene within the body. The other strand is believed to be there to stabilise the template / sense strand although it too contains some genetic code. I put forward that this "stabilising" strand is the soul or life force.

Each strand of the double helix within the DNA molecule contains different genes. The genes on the template / sense strand are called on first when the body needs to heal itself. However the stabilising strand is capable of acting as the template / sense strand providing the enzymes that transcribe the DNA are activated. Healing to a greater or lesser degree usually takes place under "normal" circumstances. However there are other cases, including those cases where there has been great trauma. I put forward that true spiritual healing works by activating the stabilising strand, which is really the soul in us. One energy successfully activates another.

I put forward that the heart is the centre from which prayer and communication should be sent and received. Prayer said from the heart with good intent will always be answered although it might not be possible for it to be activated immediately or in the way asked for. This is because other actions are simultaneously at work and could have been at work in the form of vibrations / energy to cause the situation initially. They might have to be worked through first. God never prevents good happening but on the earth nothing is purely good. God is always there but bad and evil coexist with good.

To get the desired reaction or result from an experiment or anything there has to be the right balance of everything to initiate it. In other words the preparation is vital. The quantities and order of the substances to create a successful experiment have to be exact. In the same way the quantities and order, or rather just what led to causing the situation determines the outcome. Results are the sum of whatever went before and sometimes it takes years or a lifetime to reach the request couched in prayer. The more involved a situation is, the longer it will take to disentangle all the strands of it and answer that prayer. Everything is vibration or energy however it is manifested. Solids, liquids and gases: thoughts, deeds and actions are all included. A prayer is a vibration set in motion into the atmosphere. It has to work through all the other energies that created the situation in question.

Curses are "prayers" for evil or bad to happen. If the energy behind them is strong enough they can work.     However, they do not stop there. Momentum carries them on and some time in the future they find their way back to the sender.  The worst thing about that for whoever sent them, is that bad and evil energy in the form of vibrations become attached to the original curse, making it many times stronger when it does return.

## Reaping what you Sow or Karma (showing what you really are)

Thoughts, words and deeds all need energy to manifest and then produce energy when manifesting. Bad thoughts can lead to bad actions and wrong doings.
St Matthew in chapter 12 verse 35 quotes Jesus as saying,

*"A good man out of the good treasures of the heart bringeth forth good things: and an evil man out of the evil treasure bringeth forth evil things"*

Even if the bad thoughts are shut off at source it is still energy going out into the atmosphere. In this case, though, the bad thoughts are neutralised or balanced by the following good thoughts. Words that are deliberately used to hurt or harm another are damaging, and will cause harm to the giver. It is the same with wrong doings. Consciously and deliberately harming another person or creature will bring that suffering on oneself, but many times worse.

The Ten Commandments were given as a code for living in a community. The threat of punishment was given for disobedience against the commands to accept God as the only god, to love Him, and not to take His name in vain, Exodus chapter 20 verses 3 to 7. The remaining commandments were simply instructions to live by the rule of doing unto others what you would like done to you. You should not kill, you should not lie and you should not steal anything including someone else's partner. That is what adultery is. Killing, lying, and stealing generate a series of events that unbalance society and create victims who suffer. However, much suffering will also find the perpetrator in the future through divine or spiritual law. Some term it karma, but it is simply a balancing act that happens as a reaction to an action, the response to anything done by anyone. In the Bible, the book of Job, chapter 4, verse 8 states,

*"they that plow iniquity, and sow wickedness, reap the same"*

and Galations chapter 6 verse7 says,

*"Be not deceived; God is not mocked: for whatsoever a man soweth, that shall he also reap."*

Additionally, desire for things that belong to others should be controlled. This is because it could lead to killing or stealing. If you can not get what you want by honest work or circumstance then you should accept the situation. Feeling resentful creates negative energy. Resentment is a bad vibration that attracts harm to whoever is resentful. As a result, whoever is resentful will get misfortune to pour down on them.

God knows people are fallible and that there is evil in the world coexisting with the good.

While one should not kill, if killing is the **only** way to stop a crazy person from murdering people then it can be condoned. The motive behind any action is most important. However, the command not to kill has always been associated with humans killing humans although there was no such limitation given in the commandment yet "Adam and Eve" were made vegan. They were instructed to eat only herbs (plants), seeds (which include nuts), and fruits. (Genesis, chapter 1 verse 29) However, their descendants, with permission from God after the Flood, were allowed meat which involved the killing of animals. Most people who had evolved killed creatures and ate them.

Stealing is wrong because it, too, unbalances society. However, if a society has developed where a small group has great wealth, allowing them plenty to eat and extremely comfortable living conditions at the expense of the majority, who are forced to live in great poverty and at subsistence or starvation level, the society is wrong. It is unbalanced and as such stealing is a symptom not a sin. However, to want what you have not got without justification for wanting it, or needing it beyond jealousy, laziness or challenge is wrongfully stealing.

Adultery can cause enormous emotional pain and suffering as well physical suffering. It is stealing someone else's partner. However, if a relationship has genuinely got bad enough for a partner to be looking elsewhere then the relationship was broken before adultery took place. There are habitual philanderers though, who should be known for what they are, and that is a very different situation. The problem or key issue is that adultery causes misery and unbalances society. Most societies do not accept it and are harsher on women because they bear the next generation. To societies that pass material wealth from generation to generation it is particularly important that both parents are known. Additionally, pregnancy and menstruation generally limit women's sexual availability to their partner which has made some men feel justified in finding temporary partners. Finally the spin that was attached to the creation story and the expulsion of Adam and Eve from Eden placed more guilt onto Eve.

Adultery is traditionally understood as breaking a marital relationship by having a sexual relationship with someone else. However, in the Bible, God does not instruct people to marry or threaten them if they do not. He wants them to choose a partner and be faithful to that partner because He is aware of the unhappiness that can be felt by someone through loneliness and sexual unfulfilment, or from rejection. That is combining Genesis chapter 2 verses18 and 24 with Exodus chapter 20 verses 14 and 17, the creation story with the Ten Commandments with an open mind, no preconditioned thinking.

Our knowledge and understanding of God the Creator comes primarily from the Bible. Genesis and the creation story tell of how a special people were made for a special job. It continues by relating stories about lives of subsequent generations and the major events of that family. There were already people on the earth living in a way that they had developed which seemed to them the most appropriate for the conditions they lived under and the understanding they had. One of the rituals that had been developed was marriage. There were different customs, including that of polygamy. This is one custom that descendants of Adam and Eve practised. Jacob, Solomon and David, from whom Jesus was descended, were polygamous. Once out of Eden, Adam and Eve were like any immigrants who had to adapt to a new environment and culture. The stoic belief in One God is what bonded the key figures and is the heritage of the Jewish nation. However, many times in the Old Testament, prophets chastise the Israelites for following the ways of neighbouring peoples too closely. The prophets main concern was that the one God, the invisible God of their fathers, was not forgotten.

The creation story that has been relayed for millennia states that Adam took the woman that was made from his rib and made her his sexual partner. Later he called her Eve. There was no

marriage ceremony of any sort.   There was no
instruction to marry.    There was no command
against adultery either, that did not come until
Moses and the Ten Commandments many
generations later.  The reason for Adam and Eve
being expelled from Eden was given as
disobedience to God.       However there was
implication that sex and nakedness were sinful.
Similarly, the blessing that was given to the newly
created male and female humans has been
accepted as a marriage ceremony although no
word of marriage or being faithful to each other
were mentioned.   If marriage as a ceremony or
institution was important to God it is a strange
omission.   The word wife was given to a woman
who had become a sexual partner.    It was to
distinguish her from a virgin.   The words spoken
were a blessing to be able to reproduce and
instructions for the special job that the created
humans were to do.  It was hoped and anticipated
that because of how Adam and Eve were made
they would be happy to be and to stay together,
Genesis chapter 2 verses 18 and 23.   The creation
story was passed on by word of mouth for possibly
a thousand years before being written down.   By
then, some of the culture and customs created and
developed by the people who were already on the
earth had become integrated with their own
inherited understandings.    The word "wife" to
explain Eve's status after her sexual relationship
with Adam is evidence of this.   If she had not been
termed Adam's wife she would have been
considered having illicit sex.   Through Adam and

Eve the Jewish people were extremely concerned about "sexual sin". Christians and Moslems inherited this.

The preceding Biblical statement obviously had a post Eden understanding attached to it as well. It appears to be an addition.

*"that a man shall leave his father and his mother, and shall cleave unto his wife and they shall be one flesh."* Genesis chapter 2 verse 24.

Adam and Eve had no parents! This statement refers to generations subsequent to Adam and Eve.

The story of the Garden of Eden is remarkably intact after millennia but it does bear witness to some adaption, apart from the fact that there are two accepted but different creation stories placed together.

Additionally, verse 14 of chapter 1 in Genesis states that the lights in the firmament of heaven, in other words, the stars and planets in the sky,

*"be for signs and for seasons, and for days and for years,"*

which seems a directive to practice astrology and monitor time. There was no directive from God to do these things and evolved mankind already practised astrology and seasonal time keeping, just as evolved mankind invented marriage.

## Unseen Forces

Superstition is based on fear. If you do not know how or can not understand why something happens it can be unnerving or miraculous. To people who have some scientific and technical knowledge, even if it is basic, the wonders of nature and technology are rationalised, and there is less place for superstition. Natural phenomena such as eclipses, tornadoes, earthquakes, volcanic eruptions or the aurora borealis are recognised to a greater or lesser degree for what they are, as is conception and birth.

The level of knowledge that science has reached is great enough for the filtered down versions to dispel much fear and superstition. However, there are still areas where superstition is still held. These include death and religion. It is because these cannot be fully and rationally understood that they are partly conceptualised and therefore open to fear and superstition.

Death is a fact of life, but what happens after death, beyond physical decay? Although religion answers this question, faith is needed to believe what religion says. A further problem is that some of what religion has taught, most notably that Adam and Eve were the first man and woman on earth, does not withstand scientific evidence. Also what has followed on from that teaching has become increasingly questionable. Additionally, with a long history of persecuting scientists for valid new knowledge about the world, the universe and the human body, the Church held fast to increasingly outdated understandings. As a result, many people feel that the Church cannot be fully believed or trusted.

Faith is something personal that one either has or does not have and one does not have to attend Church to sustain it. Faith is not dependent on knowledge either. If science learns more about our world it is evident that it and all of life is more incredible than previously appreciated. New truths are new parameters. They should not affect faith because faith is something completely different. However, when faith is so tied to history, geography or the sciences that it cannot be separated from them, there is a problem. Academic knowledge changes. It is dependent on many factors. Faith and true religion are not academic. Faith is something that people carry inside themselves as a belief in some greater power beyond this world. It is intangible. It is hard to describe without the use of words employed by religion. Even with these words it might not be easy. Anyway true religion is believing in a higher power of good and trying to be the best person one can be, that is, treating other people how you would want to be treated. If everyone did this, the world would be a better place and true religion would be fulfilled because everything else written about in religion is amplification of those two premises.

Jesus said,

*"Thou shalt love the Lord thy God with all thy heart, and with all thy soul and with all thy mind. This is the first and great commandment.   And the second is like unto it, Thou shalt love thy neighbour as thyself.        On these two commandments hang all the law and the prophets."*
(St. Matthew chapter 22 verses 37 – 40)

The "law" referred to are the laws governing the Jewish way of life as laid down in the Torah. These were intended to help a person lead a life the way God intended.   Prophets arose trying to keep the Jewish people on track religiously and morally.   Sage and Rabbi of the early Rabbinic period, Hillel the Elder, c. 1B.C.E. – 1C.E. who became head of Palestinian Jewry is reputed to have said that the Torah could be summed up as follows,

*"What is hateful to you do not do to your fellow. The rest is commentary on this."*

(Dictionary of Jewish Law and Legend.  Thames and Hudson Ltd., London.  Reprinted 1998.  Alan Unterman.  Page 94)

Rabbi Akiva, a second century Mishnaic sage, agreed with Hillel.   He said that the great principle of the Torah was based on the statement in verse 18 of chapter 19 in Leviticus, *"love your neighbour as yourself"*.

(Dictionary of Jewish Law and Legend. Ibid. Page 200)

Both Hillel and Akiva as devout Jews, would have recited the shema in their morning and evening prayers. The shema includes the affirmation that,

*"thou shalt love the Lord thy God with all thine heart and with all thy soul and with all thy might."*

(Deuteronomy chapter 6 verse 5) and

*"if ye shall hearken diligently unto my commandments which I command you this day, to love the Lord your God, and to serve him with all your heart and with all your soul, that I will give you the rain of your land in his due season, ---."*

(Deuteronomy chapter11 verses13 and 14)

To devout Jews there was no question that God comes first.

Practising Moslems believe similarly, and in their Qur'an, Sura 4 verse 36, the English translation reads,

*"Worship Allah and join none with Him (in worship); and do good to parents, kinsfolk, orphans, the poor, the neighbour who is near of*

*kin, the neighbour who is a stranger, the
companion by your side, the wayfarer, and those
whom your right hand possesses - -.*"

The fundamental belief of Islamic monotheism is
summed up in the Tauhid, their statement of faith.

All three monotheistic religions accept that there is
one God who should be worshipped, loved,
respected and revered with one's whole being.
They also state, in their own way, that one should
treat others as you want to be treated.

However superstition has become attached to
much of religion. As a result clothes and foods are
regulated and it is taboo if certain practices are not
performed. These are customs and some date
back before the religion now practised was
observed. They have become attached to, and
identified with, the religion. Reasons are given for
continuing them based on scripture.

There is a belief that has developed within
Christianity which confuses both Jews and
Moslems. Devout Christians believe that Jesus is
the Son of God and that as such, God came down
to earth. He is their Messiah. While Jews cannot
accept Jesus at all, Moslems can. Moslems also
revere Jesus as a prophet with elevated status, but
not with divinity. To Moslems and Jews there is
strictly only one God. God cannot be divided or
have any one share his place. The concept of the
Trinity is anathema to them. It is something that

Jews and Moslems perceive as impossible if one believes in One God which Christians also claim.

Many Christians find the Trinity a difficult concept but accept it because the Church declares it. However, the concept was not defined or made doctrine until the mid three hundreds – about three and half centuries after Jesus died. Why? Because it was in the fourth century that Christians started to seriously debate whether Jesus was God come down to earth or a man.

Before 311 Christians had to survive persecutions. Then in 311, Galerius, the emperor of the eastern region of the Roman Empire, decided to issue an edict allowing Christians to hold their religious assemblies, provided that they did nothing to disturb the public order. This turnabout happened because Galerius realised persecution had failed to curb the Christians who had instead, become "hardened" to them. As a result of Galerius's edict, Christianity was officially identified as a religion and allowed to practice openly. This then led some Christians to want to define their religion.

One year later, in 312 Constantine won the Battle of Milvian Bridge and became Roman Emperor. Shortly afterwards he declared himself a Christian because he believed he had won through divine help. Constantine had been convinced he saw the sign of the cross in the sky before the battle and responded by ordering his soldiers to put a cross on their shields.　　As time went by, he gave Christians more state support that further strengthened their position.

Discussions and arguments increased as to whether Jesus was God or a man.　Then in 325 C.E., at the Council of Nicea, the Church concluded that Jesus was "of one substance" with God.　The repercussion of this was to challenge the previous understanding of God which then had to be redefined.　This was further complicated because some Christians accepted that the Holy Spirit was another functioning part of God.　The final outcome of all the debates was to formulate a term to express this new understanding of God. In this way the Trinity was devised.　The belief was confirmed at the Council of Chalcedon in 451 C.E.

# Death

Energy cannot be destroyed but it can change. There is only a finite amount of energy in the universe. For that reason there is a maximum of life that the world can support. The maximum is regulated by the environment. Wrong interference with nature will cause natural disasters. Death does not mean the extinction of life but a change of existence.

To people with an open mind or a belief in ghosts, ghosts are evidence that life exists in other forms. I suggest that ghosts are real, and to ghosts, their world is just as authentic as our world is to us. The explanation I understand and accept for this is that they exist on a different frequency level or vibration than humans. This makes it harder for everyone to see them. If the widest spectrum for human vision is measured on a scale of 1 – 10 and most people see within the range of 2 – 8, those with clairvoyant abilities can see more of the spectrum. Equally there are sounds that are known to exist but cannot be heard by people. For example, dogs can hear higher notes than humans, which is proved by the dog whistle. However, they do not hear some of the low notes humans can hear. Similarly, insect repellents have been devised that work on high pitched sound which humans are unable to hear. Additionally, radio and television sounds and pictures travel through the air unheard and unseen by us but can be gathered and disseminated by appropriate equipment that picks them up on the relevant frequencies as vibrations and then translates them into sounds and pictures we can see, hear and understand. That is what radios and televisions do. I believe ghosts exist on a higher frequency than earthly life. As a result the atoms and molecules from which they are composed move at a faster rate, and are more dispersed. It is this that makes them harder to see. It also enables them to walk through walls or closed doors as some people claim to have seen. Walls and doors are solid items to us because their molecules are packed densely and vibrate very slowly. Ghosts being composed of molecules vibrating at a higher frequency can move between the molecules of what we perceive as a solid object so are therefore able to go through walls and doors on earth.

All mainstream, and many other religions, acknowledge spirits. To them, "spirits" are a form of energy, disembodied from the physical body. While the words "spirit" and "spiritual" are usually associated with some form of religion or belief system, the words "ghost" and "ghostly" are not, with the notable exception of the Holy Ghost in Christianity. However, this too is an expression of disembodied energy or "power". It is power that belongs to God and is therefore "supernatural".

## The Power and The Glory

As stated before, everything that exists in the universe is an expression of energy. There are two forces of that energy: positive and negative. Both are necessary but they need to be in balance to be harmless. Positive energy is good and also the creative energy of the universe, negative energy is potentially the bad and in its uncontrolled form, evil. Negative energy cannot create and ultimately destroys itself and anything attached to it if it becomes too powerful. It needs positive energy to exist but positive energy needs negative energy to fully express itself. The universe is finite and it is a living body. The earth is a molecule in that body. Just as beneficent and harmful microbes live on the molecules in the human body so people live on the earth good and bad together.

Energy is constantly active in one form or another. The basic or cellular level of energy in the universe creates everything in the universe. It is invisible to the human eye but a charge can be seen as a spark and what we call lightning is an electric storm. This energy has powers of attraction and repulsion.

An electric current occurs when the electrons in an atom move. Electricity can be produced directly from heat, pressure or light. Electric current flows because a force acts on the electrons. If the force causes there to be more or less electrons in the atom the remaining electrons can attract or repel.    The aura of a person is the electrical current generated from their body.    The aura attracts good or bad from what it generates because what it gives out attracts energy back. Religion acknowledges haloes.   That is part of the aura.

God and Satan are really the ultimate forces yet their names have come from religion.    As the basics of electricity, atomic science and DNA were discovered and developed, religion was not sought for explanations or terminology.    Science and religion had already become two totally different disciplines because the Church did not want established religion challenged.    If what the Church teaches is true it should not fear questions. Unfortunately when challenges to the Church's teaching came up in the past, it vehemently denied everything that was different from the scriptures and quoted scripture should not be changed in any way.

Quotes from the Bible are still thrown out by some, in an attempt to keep the understanding contained in it at a pre-medieval level.   The problem is that people's minds, understanding and education have moved on centuries.    Fear, fines, ostracism and torture were used to suppress questions until the questions were on so many people's minds and lips that it was inevitable the Church's authority in some intellectual disciplines and in certain geographical areas was crushed.   The Church discredited itself by the way it defended itself.

Although the Church appeals to fewer people many people want to be able to believe in something spiritual. Many people accept that there is an aspect of life that is only explainable in some form of spiritual dimension. The emergence of the New Age Movement and the open and increased practice of Paganism, Witchcraft and Animism show this. There are also people who look up to successful personalities who have made a great deal of money as icons, and for them, shopping could be likened to a religious ritual. Updating priests' robes, changing Latin or Old English to a modern vernacular, or bringing in a few guitars to play modern tunes to modern hymns, is not the answer to entice large numbers of people back to Church. Credibility with spiritual fulfilment is needed, something that is both plausible and mystical.

The Bible, and especially the teaching Jesus gave, forms the basis of eternal truth and can stand up to any amount of analysis *providing* the understanding attached to some of the verses is not the same as the one of thousands of years ago. The spiritual essence is true so will stand up to intense scrutiny since ultimate truth always does. However, while the basic needs of life have always been the same, mankind's expectations and understanding of the world and the universe are totally different from Biblical times and from the period Jesus lived on Earth. Just as measurements and currency have changed form, the ways to express things through words has altered. Language evolves. It evolves to express the changes in the way of life. From sanitation, medicine and cooking, to transport by donkey to spaceships on the moon.

The writers Chaucer, Shakespeare and Dickens only span approximately five hundred years and yet their "English", expression of it, and understanding of the world is vastly different from each other. They are still considered great writers although it is necessary to have some background knowledge to appreciate their work fully because life including speech and understanding has changed so much. However, despite the basic requirements of life remaining the same and truth being the truth, there is a proviso. The truth can be limited to knowledge of a situation. When scientific discoveries are made, understanding is increased, and a previous boundary broken down. In this way what was believed "truth" before has been disproved, so is no longer the truth on a particular issue. It is not that anyone lied. This is what has happened to the Bible. It was written by and for people who had limited or no scientific knowledge. Similarly their knowledge of world geography was restricted. They tried to express spiritual truth in the best way they could, but it was using a vocabulary and mindset of the times and circumstances under which they wrote. The way of life, as well as expectations and understanding of life, have changed dramatically over time. Thousands of years have elapsed since the Creation Story was first recorded with some other scriptural stories, and during that time people' perception has changed enormously. The spiritual content is ultimate truth but in imparting it to people the words need to be expressed in a way people can understand and in a setting they can relate to. It has to be credible. Initially the Church did not appreciate this, then was slow to act and did so in a very restricted way. Printing Bibles in modern languages has not been enough for many people. Though people of faith can lift out the spiritual truths and appreciate them, understanding is limited as the Bible stands. Parts of the Old Testament do not seem plausible any more. The result of this and of alternative religions being taught with equal emphasis, has made many people lack knowledge of, or interest in, the Bible. There is much that needs explaining because previous boundaries have been broken.

The new understandings or parameters have not made the Bible obsolete. The truths need to be lifted out and put with updated knowledge for the Bible to be properly understood within a scientific world. Spirituality is timeless, history, geography and the sciences change with increased knowledge. The Bible's parameters on most subjects are outdated. However, the most important subject, that of God, holds true. Since religion and spirituality should be the key reason for the Bible and scripture, it should not matter that historical, geographical and scientific knowledge of the world is far advanced from that of thousands of years ago.  God is the Creator of the universe, our world and us.  That is the basic tenet and it has not changed, it cannot change.  If everyone treated others as they would like to be treated, laws and commandments would be made obsolete. However, Judaism and Christianity are guilty of clinging to almost prehistoric knowledge, maintaining they are beliefs, just to maintain the integrity of the belief that God is the Creator.  It is possible to acknowledge all that God is, while at the same time appreciating the increased knowledge and understanding people have been given.  If properly used this would enable all humans to live healthier and more comfortable lives.  God is behind all knowledge that helps mankind and His world, but He wants it to be used fairly.  As always though, good brings the potential of evil in its wake.  Evil brings greed into the equation and many suffer as a consequence. Throughout history many have suffered through the greed of others, but that is not an excuse to continue in the same way.  It should be a reason for all mankind to improve in another direction, spiritually.

Our world the Earth was created within an existing universe and is an integral part of it.  All the mainstream religions believe that "God" is the Creator of our world, the universe and everything in it, and Judaism, Christianity and Islam tell their own version in Genesis in the Torah, Pentateuch, and Bible as well as various surahs in the Qur'an.

God is believed to be omnipotent and omnipresent and yet cannot be seen. Believers have faith and can feel His presence. Many accept that spiritual healing does happen and that God communicates to the people of Earth through prophets, angels and even supernatural phenomena.

Energy is generated by and in the universe. Thoughts, words and deeds all need energy to manifest, and when manifest, the energy created goes out into the universe and does not stop until it finds and binds with receptive existing energy. There is a chain of energy which forms a circle, eventually replacing the energy first used.

## Fall-Out from the Sky

When a white hole emits elements into the atmosphere it also emits a high level of radiation. There is still radiation in the atmosphere now after the last white hole emission, although it is at a much lower level. The remains of the "fall out" can be seen on a T.V. as a percentage of the white flecks that show when the T.V. is between channels. Obviously the nearer to the fall-out and the closer in time to the emission, the stronger the radiation is, because through distance and with time the radiation spreads increasingly into the atmosphere. However, this radiation has been important in the development of this world and the universe. Historically, when there has been a surge of atmospheric radiation fallout it has led to changes and mutations where it drops most densely. These changes subsequently spread across the world.

Although nature has produced genetic changes, industrial waste, specifically nuclear, in the twentieth century caused many dramatic mutations of a different kind, in a comparatively short time. Some authorities are trying to redress this damage. In the past, radiation from beyond the earth caused changes when it dropped into the earth's atmosphere. I put forward that for this reason the dinosaurs became extinct and ape-man evolved. Evolved ape-man who had been roaming across much of the world's land mass inexplicably became our ancestor when large amounts of another fall-out descended over the area of the Middle East and North Africa. I put forward there is no "missing link": there was mutation. For this reason civilisation as we know it began in what was Mesopotamia about 4000 B.C.E. It was why God decided to have the Garden of Eden there at that time and to create humans whom he hoped would intermarry with the existing humans whereby increasing their spiritual understanding and potential. That plan did not work out exactly as formulated but it is succeeding in a modified way.

# In the Beginning

The couple we know as Adam and Eve were expelled from Eden but took with them knowledge and guilt which they passed down.  The Old Testament is their story and the history of their descendants.  At times it was couched in words that were metaphorical and it always appeared that parochial events were world events.  To the people involved they were world events because they happened in their world and they knew little or nothing beyond their area.  There was no global conception.

Why had Adam and Eve been expelled from Eden? Jews and Christians emphasise that Eve tempted Adam to disobey God's command to leave untouched the fruit on the tree of the knowledge of good and evil.    Interestingly, although Islam acknowledges that story, it does not emphasise it. For generations after the events in the Creation Story, people have questioned what the fruit was. While it was reckoned that Adam and Eve were created in 4004 B.C.E. and the first stories passed down by word of mouth, the oldest parts of the Hebrew Bible were not written down until around 3000 years later, in approximately 1000 B.C.E. Jesus was born around 1000 years later and Islam was founded around 600 years after that.

Because Adam and Eve were expelled from Eden certain key figures like Noah and Abraham were singled out to continue the purpose of Adam and

Eve's creation because they were more aware of God and the spiritual dimension of life. Noah and his family were kept alive during a great flood in their area so that Abraham could later be born into that family. Abraham is the man that the Jews acknowledge as the Father of their race. In reality, their race started with Adam and Eve.

Although there were other men and women created they were not expelled from Eden, so after Eden, Adam and Eve had no contact with the others. It seems that there was contact with the being they called "God" though, by at least Able and Cain.

The story of Adam and Eve in the Garden of Eden is a mixture of truth and metaphor which I interpret in the following way. Adam and Eve were created, but by God's representatives. In passing down their story they called the leader of their makers and teachers, "God", and said they, Adam and Eve, were the first man and woman on earth. They were the first out of Eden not the first inhabitants of the world. Interestingly, Jesus speaks about *"he that made them"* when referring to "God" making Adam and Eve. St Matthew chapter 19 verse 4. Adam and Eve also related simply the creation of our world and its solar system. We now understand this scientifically. The tree of the knowledge of good and evil and the tree of life are metaphors. God's representatives were termed by Adam and Eve in their story as the "tree of life" because God is the Creator.

Whenever and wherever God works, the "Evil One"
tries to get in on the act and stop Him.   Eden was
no exception.    In fact because this was such an
important spiritual exercise or project, there were
also people owing allegiance to the "Evil One" in
the Garden.   This was embodied evil energy and it
counterbalanced the embodied good energy, "the
representatives of God".   Adam and Eve used the
metaphor "tree of the knowledge of good and evil"
to describe the "Evil One's" followers.      The
"serpent" another metaphorical name, was their
leader, Satan.      The understanding of this
metaphor has been standardly accepted.   The men
created were given a partner who was a women
cloned from themselves although they did not have
to choose her as a sexual partner.   They were told
in Genesis chapter 2 verses 16 and 17 that they
could eat the fruit of any tree in the garden except
that from the tree of the knowledge of good and
evil.   In other words they could choose to have a
sexual relationship with any of the created women
but  not  any  of  the  "Evil  One's"  female
representatives.   Adam chose to be with Eve.   A
little later Eve was tempted to have sex with Satan,
termed the serpent in the story.   She did not have
difficulty in getting Adam to have sex with one of
Satan's females afterwards.    Genesis chapter 3
verses 1 to 7.  Was not this adultery?
Following this, God said to Eve,

*"what is this that thou hast done?"*

She replied,

*"the serpent beguiled me, and I did eat."*

There was punishment in addition to being expelled from Eden. Both were affected. In Genesis chapter 3 verses 16 to 19 God to Eve,

*"I will greatly multiply thy sorrow and thy conception; in sorrow shalt thou bring forth children; and thy desire shall be to thy husband, and he shall rule over thee."*

To Adam God said,

*"cursed is the ground for thy sake; in sorrow shalt thou eat of it all the days of thy life; thorns also and thistles shall it bring forth to thee; and thou shalt eat the herb of the field; in the sweat of thy face shalt thou eat bread, till thou return unto the ground; for out of it wast thou taken: for dust thou art and unto dust thou shalt return."*

Jewish folklore and legend tells of Adam being with Lileth a demoness of Satan before he was with Eve. It also accepts that Eve was made pregnant by Satan, the "serpent", and as a result was expelled from Eden with Adam. The baby conceived was to become Cain. The emphasis on sex being sinful stems from Adam and Eve's sexual activity with Satan and his partners. Eve was blamed because if she had not had sex with "Satan" and become pregnant by him they would not have been forced to leave Eden. Not a story that they would want to repeat transparently, but a story that needed to be repeated with some semblance of truth if they wanted to explain themselves and atone for the wrong they did. We owe the knowledge of the One God to Adam and Eve and the conviction of those descendants who also believed. Jesus was born into the Jewish race because of this. He came to try and redirect the Jews back onto their original path. However, as a race the Jews rejected Jesus whose teaching simplified the Jewish Law in a remarkable and inspiring way. It was the gentiles or evolved humans who showed more interest in Jesus.

Satan is mentioned in the Bible and is considered the epitome of evil, but he is not. Pure evil is much more powerful and can not be contained fully on the earth just as God is beyond the confines of the earth. However, just as the power of creation and the life force on earth are from God, pure evil is in the world but its energy can only be expressed fully out of it. Jesus is the human embodiment of God's power on earth, Satan is the human embodiment of evil on the earth.

There is a name for pure evil or the "Evil One" but it should never be used because using it brings evil energy to the user. Everything is energy good or bad. The Jews have inherited a belief and fear in using God's name but there is no harm in using it providing it is not done in a blasphemous way.

Using God's name properly brings good energy and blessings.

## Homosexuality

Homosexuality has been severely punished by those following monotheistic religions. It has enraged people and been considered a perversion because it was believed that God intended a man to have a sexual relationship with a women not another man. It was also believed and preached that a union between a man and a women should produce children. There was stigma and shame if this did not happen, and for Jews, a cause for divorce. Both Jews and Christians taught that birth control was sinful. Today this still applies to some branches of practising Jews and Christians. "Be fruitful and multiply"
Genesis chapter, 1 verse 28.

So, traditionally homosexuality was condemned because it has been believed and taught that,

a)    God made woman for man
b)    God commanded mankind to multiply and replenish the earth – in other words have lots of children
c)    A single sex relationship contravenes the first and cannot provide the second

This teaching has been fundamental. But why?

Christian tradition has its roots in Judaism. The "Jewish " family knew that in their beginning, their God had made woman for man and that they were to "be fruitful and multiply". For these reasons they would not tolerate homosexuality. It was necessary for the Jewish family's purpose to be heterosexual.  However, just as certain animals evolved with different sexual preferences, so did the human animal.  It is a genetic thing which should also make the accepted homosexual and bisexual relationships of the ancient world better understood, especially those in Greece and the Roman Empire.  The difference was with the Jewish race.  Originating from Adam and Eve, who passed on their story that man was created by God and woman was made for him, Judaism and subsequently Christianity and Islam outlawed homosexuality.  To the Jews heterosexual relationships were a divine arrangement that could not be changed.  Adam and Eve instilled a fear of sexual wrong-doing into their descendants that not only became incorporated into Judaism but subsequently into Christianity.  Sexual sin included homosexuality.  People who were descendants of evolved humans did not have the same understanding  and did not have exactly the same genetic code.  They like some animals could inherit a gene that did not make same sex affection or relationships abnormal.  To those that are made that way it is perfectly normal.  Established monotheistic religions have not been able to accept homosexuality as normal for anyone.  However, their criterion is based on a belief that comes from a source that is no longer legitimate.

The Creation Story as related in Genesis, became the basis on which the history of the world and its inhabitants, including man, was accepted in the western world. However, when science found evidence to its own, and other peoples' satisfaction, that not only is the world and humankind much older than the theologically calculated 4004 B.C.E., but that mankind evolved, there was inevitably conflict of beliefs. Initially the Church found the scientific discoveries hard to accept. While some people of faith still do, many people of faith make compromises of some sort between the two versions. Despite this, the foundations of our cultural understanding has been based on an implicit belief in the Creation Story. In turn, the conclusions derived at from this story became beliefs, and were generated by the orthodox teaching of this story. The beliefs surround homosexuality, sexual relationships outside marriage, marriage, adultery, divorce and women's position in society.

## Marriage and Divorce

By telling us that,

*"in the resurrection they neither marry, or are given in marriage"*,

Jesus told us implicitly that marriage is an earthly institution.  Matthew chapter 22 verse 30, Mark chapter 12 verse 25, and Luke chapter 20 verse 35. When asked by the Pharisees about divorce,

*"is it lawful for a man to put away his wife for any cause?"*

Jesus replied with an answer directly from the Creation Story,

*"He that made them at the beginning made them male and female, and said, for this cause shall a man leave his father and mother, and shall cleave to his wife and they shall be one flesh?"*

Recounted in St Matthew chapter 19 verses 3 – 6 but quoted from Genesis chapter 2 verses 22 – 24.

Jesus continues by, reaffirming the last statement,

*"wherefore they are no more twain, but one flesh"*

This describes a sexual union not a marriage.  If it describes a marriage every sexual act / relationship would equally be a marriage by this definition, but they are not.  Fornication, adultery and prostitution are railed against, but equally they are "two making one flesh". It has been accepted that Adam and Eve were married but there is no evidence of marriage. Jesus, by stating the wording of the relevant Genesis verse, and then repeating it, emphasises what it really says. However Jesus then adds,

*"what God has joined together let no man put asunder"*.

This is profoundly meaningful and has had enormous impact on the Church.

In both accounts, Genesis and St Matthew's, a man shall leave his parents to cleave to his wife so they shall be one flesh. The man is not called a husband, the woman however, is called a *"wife"*. There was no marriage ceremony recorded, just a sexual union. There was no instruction given for marriage in Genesis by God, or in the Gospels by Jesus. In Genesis the words

*"be fruitful and multiply and replenish the earth"*,

are also recorded. Again that refers specifically to a sexual union. The Ten Commandments and the Laws of Moses make no mention of a marriage ceremony ordained by God. This is despite other commands and instructions being given. While there is no commandment to marry or divorce, there is a commandment that says not to commit adultery and the statement by Jesus,

*"what God has joined together let no man put
asunder".*

As stated earlier there was evolved man and
created man. It has been recorded in the Bible
that God sent prophets to the Jewish people to
keep them on track. Although the most important
thing for the Jewish people was to keep true to
their God, it was known they copied certain ways
of life from the surrounding tribes. It seems that
one of the absorbed customs was marriage. When
they came to write down their history after
transmitting it orally for generations it was felt
necessary to call Eve *"wife"* after the sexual union.
Genesis chapter 2, verse 24. That way there was
no stigma attached to the sexual relationship.
Additionally verse 24 appears to be appended to
the original story that breaks between verse 23 and
25 to accommodate it.

Polygamy was mentioned in the Bible and
practised by some of the most important Jewish
characters, including Jacob, Solomon and David.
Subsequent wives were not spoken of as being
taken in adultery although the relationship of
Adam and Eve appears to be a monogamous one
after Eden and has been used as an example for
future relationships. This is despite adultery
being defined as a subsequent sexual union, within
or without marriage, when both the original sexual
partners are still alive. Also, although concubines
do not have the same status as wives they are not
called adulterous relationships. Solomon, who

according to the Bible had seven hundred wives and three hundred concubines, was not accused of adultery. He was accused of building altars to false gods, gods of his wives, and not being true to the One God. 1 Kings chapter11 verses 3 – 10. It appears that polygamy was a different marriage custom copied.

Arranged marriages were not ordained by God either but have been practised for thousands of years and many are recorded in the Bible. Although Solomon had an excessive number of wives, there were social reasons for polygamy and arranged marriages. However, as good as the original intentions might have been for such arrangements, abuses are possible and a marriage where there is no love / physical attraction contravenes God's initial intention and instruction in Genesis. It also allows the sexual needs of the unfulfilled person to be prey to covetousness or lust and to commit adultery if there was the inclination or opportunity. In 1 Corinthians chapter 7 verses 3 – 5 there are clear instructions to the husband and the wife not to defraud the other sexually. There are also instructions for the husband to love his wife in Ephesians chapter 5 verse 25, 28 and 33 and the wife to love her husband in Titus chapter 2 verse 4.

Divorce is the word used to describe a dissolved union of marriage. Jesus says divorce does not stop adultery taking place if the ex husband and / or the ex wife remarry. St Matthew chapter 19 verse 9. Only death of the ex partner releases one from committing adultery if one goes into another sexual relationship. But then there must only be one physical relationship or adultery is committed. However, Jesus also says specifically to the men,

*"Ye have heard that it was said by them of old time, Thou shalt not commit adultery, But I say unto you, That whosoever looketh on a woman to lust after her hath already committed adultery with her in his heart."*

He continues to them,

*"if thy right eye offend thee, pluck it out, and cast it from thee: for it is profitable for thee that one of thy members should perish, and not that thy whole body should be cast in hell. And if thy right hand offend thee, cut it off, and cast it from thee - - -."*

St Matthew chapter 5 verse 27 to 31.

By contrast and balance, St John chapter 8 verses 4 to 11, tells of a woman taken in the act of adultery and brought to Jesus. The scribes and Pharisees who brought her said that the Law of Moses commanded them to stone her but they wanted to know what Jesus would say. Jesus' reply was,

*"he that is without sin among you, let him first cast a stone at her".*

One by one all the men left leaving only Jesus with the woman. Jesus then said to her,

*"where are those thine accusers?    Hath no man condemned thee?"*

The woman replied that none now did.   Jesus then said,

*"neither do I condemn thee: go, and sin no more".*

Paul states in the Bible that the Law, referring to the Jewish Law or the Law of Moses, makes people aware that they sin, so conversely if there was no Law, that is Jewish Law, lust, covetousness and adultery would not be sinful.   Romans chapter 7 verse 7.   However, in Romans chapter 3 verse 9 and 10, Paul states clearly that everyone, Jews and Gentiles are sinful.     Paul was a Jew but he converted many gentiles to Christianity.   Gentiles had always been outside the Jewish Law unless,
a) in Biblical times they were linked with or
    attached to a Jewish household in some way, or
b) converted to Christianity.

There is a "blur" here as there frequently is when religion, customs and secular authority converge. Christians absorbed the Jewish scripture from their Bible and know it as the Old Testament.   It was considered the explanation of the creation of our world, universe and everything in it. Christians do not use the Talmud or other religious writings, but Jesus was a Jew.   He came to the Jews to carry on where the prophets left off. When the "Christians" became more than a Jewish sect and a religion in their own right, it was understood that the Jewish Law was not needed to live a life God would be pleased with. Examples include, 1 Corinthians chapter 7 verse 18 and Romans chapter 2 verse 26. Jesus came to fulfil the Law but he says that it stands until it has served its purpose. St Matthew chapter 5 verses 17 and 18. The purpose of the Law was to make people aware that there is One God, Father of all and that one should treat everyone as best as one can. Jesus said,

*"Thou shalt love the Lord thy God with all thy heart, and with all thy soul, and with all thy mind. This is the first and great commandment. And the second is like unto it, Thou shalt love thy neighbour as thyself. On these two commandments hang all the Law and the Prophets."*

St Matthew chapter 22 verses 37 to 40. The first part is also stated in Deuteronomy chapter 6 verse 5 and is part of the Jewish Shema.

Paul in Romans chapter 13 verse 8 to 10 explains that love fulfils the Law.

*"Owe no man anything but to love one another: for he that loveth another hath fulfilled the Law. For this, Thou shalt not commit adultery, Thou shalt not kill, Thou shalt not steal, Thou shalt not*

*bear false witness, Thou shalt not covet; and there be any other commandment, it is briefly comprehended in this saying, namely, Thou shalt love thy neighbour as thyself. Love worketh no ill to his neighbour: therefore love is the fulfilling of the Law."*

When Jesus says that he comes to fulfil the Law, as quoted in St Matthew chapter 5, he continues by saying that the Law will not change until all is fulfilled. He then follows with an explanation. Just by observing the letter of the Law as the scribes and the Pharisees do, does not make one righteous. For example not killing is commanded but all the inferences, subtleties and nuances of anger are not. Jesus tells us that not only are they damaging but that they also endanger one's soul. St Matthew chapter 5 verses 21 to 26. St Matthew chapter 15 verse 19 and Mark chapter 7 verse 21. Similarly, not to commit adultery is a commandment but there are subtleties as described in verses 28 to 30. Adultery begins with desire and if there is desire there is lust. Jesus clamps down heavily because the men had made the Law weigh against women whereas the Commandments were unbiased. The Law of Moses allowed a woman to be stoned for adultery or divorced because her husband wanted a divorce. The Commandments did not state this. All that is stated in the Commandments is that one should not commit adultery, which means everyone.

God made humans sexual.   He is therefore aware of their sexual needs.   After understanding and appreciating what Jesus taught, Paul shows he understands the internal war between the needs of the flesh and the desire of the spirit and that in humans both are needs.   Romans chapter 7 verse 25.   Much is said about this conflict in Romans chapters 7 and 8.   John reported that Jesus did not condemn the woman committing adultery but told her not to sin any more.   John chapter 8, verse 11.   Jesus also tells us repeatedly not to judge others lest we be judged.   He also says that as we judge others so we will be judged. St Matthew chapter 7 verse 1.   Hence the men, especially the scribes and Pharisees, were in danger of condemnation even if they just lusted in their hearts but condemned a woman caught in the act of adultery.   But if she was caught in the act there must have been a sexual partner with her who was a man.

Jesus is one with the Father, St John chapter 12 verses 44 to 50, therefore what Jesus says must be what God wants.   God has committed the judging of humans to Jesus.   St John chapter 5 verse 22. Jesus will judge the living and the dead. 2 Timothy chapter 4 verse 1.   God the Spirit knows all that is in our hearts and what we need.   Romans chapter 8 verse 27.   God looks for those whose hearts and spirits change for the better.   Romans chapter 2 verse 29.

Marriage does not stop adultery. Divorce does not prevent adultery. Although man devised marriage, Paul advised marriage for those who could not remain celibate, in other words to prevent fornication. Corinthians chapter7 verses 2 and 9. One must remember that Paul was a Jew with all the cultural beliefs associated with that faith. Fornication, or sexual activity by unmarried partners, has been taught as sinful, whereas marriage has not. This is where social propriety and religious dogma blur. Church and state have looked on marriage as the correct and only way one should express sexuality. Hebrews chapter 13 verse 4. Yet neither God or Jesus ordain marriage in the Bible. Paul in 1 Corinthians chapter 7 verse 2 says,

*"to avoid fornication let every man have his own wife and let every woman have her own husband"*

but adds in verse 6,

*"I speak by permission and not by commandment".*

Jesus accepts that there is marriage but states that it is an earthly institution. Socially and historically marriage was most important for providing descendants, heirs if one was rich and had land, with both parents known. The institution also provided care for the next generation. A good marriage is a stable and enriching social benefit. A bad marriage is living hell for all involved.

God said that one should not commit adultery. To never commit adultery means to have only one sexual partner as long as both are alive. Thus the marriage of two virgins is the criterion. This is where society and Church met. However, by the definition of Jesus, neither of those two virgins should have ever had before, during or after their marriage, a sexual thought about someone other than their partner.

So if marriage is an earthly institution, and divorce a way of breaking that bond in a "social" sense, but has no spiritual standing because adultery is still being committed, it is necessary to look more at adultery.

Both God and Jesus spoke about adultery giving some definition. God said one should not commit it but did not give any threats or list punishments for committing it. By contrast God threatened with punishment those Jewish people who did not accept him as the only true God, a belief that was carried on by Christianity.

Jesus said,

*"what God has joined together let no man put asunder",*

St Matthew chapter 19 verse 6, but he does not condemn the woman taken in adultery. The statement *what God has joined together let no man put asunder* has been understood by the Church that there should be no divorce. There is a dispensation if a partner has committed adultery. However that is traditionally physical adultery only. The Church has tried to keep strictly to what was understood to be the commands of God and Jesus especially since Jesus accused the Pharisees of *"teaching for doctrines commandments of men"*.

St Matthew chapter 15 verse 8 and St Mark chapter 7 verse 7.

Jesus took the words of Isaiah chapter 29 verse 13,

*"this people* (referring to the Jews) *draw near me with their mouth and with their lips do honour me, but have removed their heart far from me, and* **their fear towards me is taught by precepts of men"**.

God wanted mankind to know him, understand him and love Him. He was aware that manmade laws had become intertwined with religion. Jesus was aware that marriage was an earthly institution. He knew that marriage had been made a religious as well as civil binding commitment and yet was not ordained by God. He appreciated that there were many kinds of marriage including those arranged for convenience where there was not necessarily any love. He was also aware that people's hearts are fallible and that people can change for the better or worse. The optimum is not to commit adultery. That is the aim. That is what God wants us to try for. But there are no punishments listed by God or Jesus for failing to manage it.

More should be understood about the preciousness of relationships and the meaning of true love as expressed by St Paul in 1 Corinthians chapter 13 although the King James version of the Bible uses the word *"charity"* instead of love.

However not only is it acknowledged that humans are sexual beings but that both partners need to have a balanced, reciprocated relationship.
1 Corinthians chapter7 verse 3 to 5.

If one truly loves God one wants to please Him. If one truly loves others as oneself, one does not want to hurt them, so should not enter into a sexual union lightly. A sexual relationship should be a precious relationship with deep feelings and care for each other. However, if it is genuinely not right despite trying hard and being patient one should not be condemned for finding a new partner. Jesus did not condemn the woman taken in adultery but told her not to do it again. He knew the circumstances just as he can see into everyone's heart. Those Jesus condemns are hypocrites and liars like those who think they are righteous by keeping the word of the commandment not to commit adultery, yet break it in their heart.   God sees into the hearts and minds of everyone.   He knows the truth so that no one can lie to Him.   If either partner does not fulfil their obligations in such a relationship they are causing a problematic situation, one in which adultery could result, mentally if not physically. Adultery is probably at least in the mind of the partner who shows no interest in the other.   It is also likely to be at least on the mind of the person who is physically neglected because of desperation. Jesus showed he knew and understood human weakness and vulnerability.

Marriage and divorce as we know it are a composite of historical Judaism, Christian understanding and secular culture.   By carefully unwinding each thread and reviewing them leads to a clearer picture of why we are, where we are, right now.

The starting point for Jewish and Christian thoughts on marriage has traditionally been with Adam and Eve. It should be noted that God provided a compatible partner for Adam and that should be the least anyone can ask for in a relationship.   Marriage is not commanded but God made humans sexual. God and Jesus understand human sexuality more than has been acknowledged. God and Jesus want people to be faithful in their relationship, or at least as far as reasonably possible.   Society used marriage, with the blessing of the Church as a sacred, inviolable institution and unquestionably the only sinless way to have a sexual relationship. This potentially benefited society in many ways but has harmed the Church.

## The Rise of Man

Judaism and Christianity have rigorously taught that mankind has fallen from grace. In other words people have become spiritually impure or defective.

Because Jesus was a Jew who came to teach Jews, Christianity inherited Jewish doctrine. It was Adam and Eve who fell from grace and were expelled from Eden. They and their descendants were spiritually impure or defective by the standard of Eden and not the descendants of evolved humans. Evolved humans were not related to Adam and Eve and their direct descendants unless they married into that line as Cain had married out of it. Jews, or Gentiles and Jews who became Christian and tried their best to lead a truly Christian life have raised themselves not fallen. Similarly descendants of evolved humans who have faithfully followed Islam have raised themselves. Descendants of evolved humans who acknowledge a spiritual side to life and try their best to live a good life by treating others as they would wish to be treated have raised themselves. People in cultures that are technologically undeveloped but who respect nature believing gods or spirits give nature its life but at the same time treat others as they would like to be treated are raising themselves up.

# Noah's Flood

The Flood described in the Bible destroyed Noah's known world, not the entire global land mass. It was an attempt to destroy the descendants of Cain who had become increasingly wicked, and those associated with them.

*"And it repented the Lord that he had made man on the earth, and it grieved him at his heart."*

That quotation was taken from Genesis chapter 6, verse 6, and relates directly to God making mankind in Genesis chapters 1 and 2. There was already evolved mankind on the earth. The Garden of Eden was a project to improve mankind by raising his spirituality. Mankind was at this time sufficiently developed to benefit from such a plan. However the plan did not work in the way hoped and subsequently needed "divine" intervention periodically. The intervention has taken various forms over the millennia from what has been perceived as miracles, to guidance from spiritually inspired people and prophets.

Noah was descended from Seth, a son born to Adam and Eve to replace Abel whom Cain killed. A new and abridged creation story starts at Genesis chapter 5 verse 1. It shows the genealogy of Seth starting with his parents, Adam and Eve. It reiterates that God created man in his likeness, that male and female were created and blessed and called Adam. Adam meaning man or mankind and from the Hebrew root word for earth. There

is no mention of Cain or Abel.  It is a new start for
the Jewish race.    The Jewish race really began
with Adam and Eve, not Abraham.   The family
despite being given several fresh starts, were still
the same family and it does not matter whether
they are called Adam and Eve and their
descendants, Canaanites, Israelites, Hebrews or
Jews.    Like all other families there are good and
bad but the difference with this one was that it was
created not evolved and was made for a special
purpose which it did not fulfil.    Hence the
disasters that befell the family throughout their
history.    The disasters were to try and put the
Jewish people back on track.

The final verses of the preceding chapter of
Genesis, chapter 4, are a bridge between the first
part of Adam and Eve's story and genealogy and
the new start.    After recounting another murder
by Cain's family it states that Adam and Eve had a
son to replace Abel. He was called Seth and in due
course became a father himself to a son.    This
bloodline reasserted God.    Cain's bloodline had
not only committed more murder as recorded in
Genesis chapter 4, verse 23, but acknowledges
vengeance and blood feud.

Some generations later Noah was born to Seth's
line.  By the time Noah was adult and had a family
of his own, the evil on earth was still increasing
and it saddened God.    Cain's bloodline had
escalated the evil on the earth, not it's spirituality,
so God allowed the evil to "self-destruct", perish

under its own impetus in a great "natural" disaster, "The Flood". However God warned Noah so that he and his family would not be drowned. That way there would be some people who had knowledge and belief of God, left alive. This was a third chance for a new start to the project. Genesis chapter 9 verse 1, starts with God blessing Noah and his sons,

*"Be fruitful and multiply, and replenish the earth".*

This is reminiscent of Genesis chapter 1 verse 22 and verse 28 and God's desire and plan for the spiritual regeneration of the world. However it has become modified. God realises that the programme has to go slower. Even Noah and his family, descendants of Adam and Eve through Seth, chosen by God to spiritually replenish the earth, and who had lived in the world before the flood, were a mixture of evolved mankind physically and culturally. The big difference was that they acknowledged God. However, now all land and sea creatures as well as birds would fear mankind because they could be considered food for mankind, Genesis chapter 9 verses 2 and 3. Both man and creatures were predators of each other, killing and defending, shedding each others blood.

There was also blood-feud. Genesis chapter 9 verse 5. Evolved mankind practised this and now the survivors of Adam and Eve's descendants did the same.    They accepted it and incorporated it into their lifestyle.      It seemed logical and reasonable to them, and for that reason, ordained by God.  Those who had displeased and disobeyed God had been killed.   Noah and his family had been saved.   Justice based on an "eye for an eye" which was so important to the Jews, was first stated.   Then it was fully and clearly restated in Exodus chapter 21 verse 24 and on two subsequent occasions, Leviticus chapter 24 verses 17 to 20 and Deuteronomy chapter 19 verse 21.

*"---Thou shalt give life for life, Eye for eye, tooth for tooth, hand for hand, foot for foot, Burning for burning, wound for wound stripe for stripe."* (Exodus chapter 21 verses 23 – 25)

Part of the original plan was for all mankind and all creatures to eventually become vegan through Adam and Eve who were only permitted to eat plants, fruits and seeds, Genesis chapter 1 verse 29.   That was all they needed to stay healthy. There was no bloodshed involved.

The other major difference, and it is really a statement, although it has been taken as either a command for, or justification for, capital punishment, is Genesis chapter 9 verse 6.

*"Whoso sheddeth man's blood, by man shall his blood be shed: - - -."*

To enforce this statement is the phrase that follows it, *"for in the image of God made he man."*

Mankind in Eden had been made in the image of those who made the people, God's representatives, not God, although the statement of belief passed down from Adam and Eve shows Noah's lineage.

Capital punishment or the death penalty is not what God intended. The world had created that punishment. It was an invention of evolved mankind and used as control and a deterrent so that the person who kills someone could expect death as punishment. The writers of Genesis had accommodated this law with much more from the culture surrounding them. It seemed to them just, for such retribution. Placing the statement,

*"for in the image of God made he man"*
immediately after

*"whoso sheddeth man's blood, by man shall his blood be shed"*,

only emphasises the strength of their belief that mankind was above all creatures and other life on earth because God made man and man was stated to be in the image of God. However, it was believed that God would want such a deterrent and punishment because the writers and readers of Genesis believed their race was special. They had forgotten that Cain was not killed for murdering his brother. God had spared his life. Killing sends out evil vibrations. Those vibrations are compounded by retaliation. Eventually evil "self destructs". Hence the coming of the Flood.

When Jesus was on Earth He taught that turning the other cheek was the better way than *"an eye for an eye"* or retaliation. Those He spoke to would be familiar with the Law – the Jewish Law or way of life. (St Matthew chapter 5 verses 38 and 39). Jesus goes on to say as quoted by Matthew in chapter 5,

*"Love your enemies, bless them that curse you, do good to them that hate you, and pray for them that despitefully use you and persecute you."*

Matthew continues, quoting Jesus saying that God sends the sun and the rain which benefits everyone, whether they are good or evil, just or unjust. Jesus says that to truly be children of our Father (God), we should therefore love everyone because there is nothing special or particularly good about loving those who love us.

## "The Others"

Although many drowned in the Flood described in the Bible, some escaped because the flood destroyed Noah's known world, not the entire land mass. There are other stories of the creation of the world and a great flood, separate and independent from those recorded in Genesis and the Qur'an. The Qur'an is the collated messages given to the Prophet Mohammed from the Angel Gabriel in the seventh century C.E. which is after the event. The stories in Genesis, which are part of Jewish and Christian scripture, date from the actual events. Noah's family are recorded survivor's who passed on the stories. The other ancient accounts or records of a great Flood and a creation story of the world were also passed down orally, then written, but by non Jewish people who had, it is believed, experienced a great flood. These other stories are called *Enuma Elish*, which is mentioned in the Pentateuch, the *Atrahasis Epic*, which is Sumerian, and the Epic of *Gilgamesh*, which is Babylonian. All were based in the Mesopotamian area.

Semitic people founded Babylon within an area known as Mesopotamia. These people came originally from Western Mesopotamia. Power struggles within Mesopotamia enabled these Western Mesopotamians to fight for independance. Once independent they became known as "Babylonians". The story of Gilgamesh had been passed down orally for many generations prior to it being written. Cain and his descendants were no longer included in the Bible as part of the "family". He had intermarried with evolved mankind, a woman from Nod, and his descendants had increasingly adapted to new ways.

Semitic people are linked by their language not their religion. Etymology which is the study of words, especially the root of the word, shows evidence of how people migrated and intermarried. There are broadly three groups of Semitic people. There are those in Mesopotamia referred to as the Eastern Semitic people, those in Northwest / West which are from Lebanon and Syria, and those from the Southwest / South of the Middle East coming from the Arabian Peninsula and Ethiopia. Akkadian, the original language of the Eastern Semites, was the language of Mesopotamia. From about 2,000 B.C.E. Akkadian subdivided into two dialects, Babylonian and Assyrian. There are three main groups of North Western Semites of which the Canaanites are one. The Canaanite group includes Phoenicians, Punic, Moabites, Edomites, Hebrews and Ammonites. Their languages were all spoken in Phoenicia as closely related languages or dialects. Phoenicians are the descendants of Canaanites.

Classical or Biblical Hebrew is known mainly from the Old Testament. Hebrew was written in the Canaanite-Phoenician alphabet until the fourth century B.C.E. when the Jews adopted Aramaic. Some time around 200 C.E. Hebrew ceased to be a spoken language but was revived for the Jews who moved to the created State of Israel in 1947.

Sanskrit is the intellectual language of both the ancient and the classical Indian civilisation. The Holy Scriptures of India, the Vedas, were compiled and written in Sanskrit after generations of oral transmission. They are a collection of religious and philosophical poems and hymns about the creation of the world and God. The philosophical and spiritual depth goes further than the Torah, Pentateuch or Old Testament. The ancient alphabet of the Indus valley is not related to Semitic but to the alphabet of the Elamites and Kushites who also came from Mesopotamia.

There were other men and women created in Eden. It was only Adam and Eve who were expelled. I put forward that those remaining completed their "training" which was to learn as much as should be passed on about God the Creator. They also had children and then migrated. Some went to India taking with them knowledge of the one God. The Vedas bares witness to their being one Supreme Being but it also shows that the one God can take many different forms. This version of monotheism is known as henotheism.

Ancient Indian civilisation dates back to around 7000 B.C.E. The existing groups of people had settled along the banks of India's northern rivers, especially the River Indus which is now in Pakistan. The sacred knowledge that was in the Vedas was brought to an existing race. It became integrated with the culture and beliefs existing in the area. Some did not like this and a serious philosophical disagreement between existing ideas and what was brought caused a social split. Those who believed and wanted to follow the Vedas stayed and became known as the Vedic people while those who disagreed moved away, further north west to an area now known as Iran. Zoroaster or Zarathushtra (c.628 – c.551 B.C.E.) came as a prophet to those people, the Iranians, and preached monotheism in a way they could understand and accept.

The Garden of Eden was home to specially created men, women and animals. They were created to improve the stock of those that had evolved on the earth by being more spiritual. The creatures were herbivores so more docile and man and woman were instructed to eat a vegan diet. Genesis chapter 1 verses 29 and 30. That way there would be no killing because killing causes bad vibrations or energy to go out into the atmosphere. Hindus who follow the Vedas are vegetarian or vegan.

The Vedas also state that the world is animated with life through electrical energy. (Rig Veda 2/43)

## Sex, Marriage and Reproduction

In Genesis it is stated that after God created the whales and other water creatures he created "winged fowls", creatures of the air or birds. He then blessed them so they could multiply or reproduce. (Genesis, chapter1, verse 22) Continuing with the list of God's creation, He then made land creatures, Genesis chapter 1, verse 25, and finally mankind in the plural, see Genesis chapter 1, verse 25. Everything was in the plural to avoid inbreeding. As He blessed the first part of the list so He blessed the second, the land creatures of which humans **are part** and included. However, additionally He instructed humans to **care** for His creation. Of all the creatures, humans have the biggest brain, and capabilities other creatures do not have.

Genetically engineered creatures and plants are sterile unless created specially to reproduce naturally. "God" has the power to create with fertility, so God's blessing on them **all** was a simplistic statement showing that God made them fertile. God did not expect future generations of whales and other sea creatures, or the birds to perform a marriage service, yet they were blessed in the same way as "Adam and Eve". No one would think of the whales, sea creatures and birds marrying, so why, when the Bible states that God blesses His land creatures, are the non-human land creatures brushed over, and it has been interpreted that the blessing shows that Adam and

Eve were the first married couple? There is no Biblical record of Adam and Eve ever being married. It has been assumed they were and preached that way to countless generations. Assumption is not evidence. Law is not based on assumptions, and trials need evidence.

Linked with this, is the belief that sex outside marriage was a heinous sin. Marriage was not commanded by God. If marriage had been a command it would have been chronicled in the Bible. Marriage was invented by evolved humans and institutionalised by religion and politics.

There is much evidence that Adam and Eve were not the first human beings on earth, some in the Bible and volumes from scientists and archaeologists. It also appears from the Creation Story and other scriptural evidence that Adam and Eve were not the only human beings created in Eden. According to the creation story more than a pair of all the other creatures were made. Adam and Eve were in that same list and spoken of in the plural. When Adam and Eve left Eden they were in disgrace for disobeying God. That does not mean they were the only humans created. The others were not accounted for in the Bible, so it was assumed and taught by subsequent generations of Jews, and later, Christians, who only had the Creation Story to go on, that Adam and Eve were the first human pair. Again, assumption is no proof. The Bible is the history of the Jews from their creation as a special people for a special purpose to the separation and establishment of a new branch of Judaism called Christianity under the most famous Jewish teacher, Jesus Christ. The strange story related and passed down from around 4004 B.C.E. was "spin doctored" by Adam and Eve for obvious reasons. But as a direct result millions of people have been misled. With all the knowledge available it is time for fact to be separated from fiction. Spirituality and true religion should stand proud for what it is, and can teach, while being strong and honest enough to separate itself from outdated history, geography and science.

# Bibliography

Cole, **K.C:** ***The Universe and the Teacup,*
Abacus, reprint 1999**
**Filkin,** David: *Stephen Hawking's Universe,*
*The Cosmos Explained*, BBC Books 1997
**Hawking,** Stephen: *The Universe in a Nutshell,*
Bantam Press, 2001
**Kugel,** James L: *The Bible As It Was,* The
Belknap Press Harvard University Press, Third
printing 1998
**McGrath,** Alister E: *Historical Theology,*
Blackwell Publishers Ltd., Oxford, UK.
**Unterman,** Alan: *Dictionary of Jewish Law and
Legend,* Thames and Hudson, reprint 1998
**Barber,** Marcus, et al: *Biology, Collins Advanced
Science,* Collins Educational,
**The Atlas of Archaeology:** Mick Aston and Tim
Taylor, Dorling Kindersley, 1998
**The Bible:** Authorised King James Version and
the Good News Bible, HarperCollins, Second
Edition 1994
**The Oxford Companion to the Bible,** edited
by Bruce M Metzger and Michael D Coogan,
Oxford University Press 1993

Internet
**Ask A Linguist 1998**; *Re Semitic Language  -
Hebrew:* http://www.linguistlist.org 2003

**Catholic Encyclopedia**
**Kashmiri Pandits**
http://ikashmir.org?Patrica/vedas.html 2003
**Linguistics:** *A quick Guide to Semitic Languages and People,* http://phoenicia.org 2003
**Triloki Nath Dhar:** *The Vedas & the Vedic Rishi: Bhagawaan Gopinath Ji* 2003
**Victoria Institute, Science and Theology Dept.** 2003
**Zarathushtra Introduction** 2003

## Author's Notes

After my husband died I became a working Mum and housewife bringing up three young children on my own. When my children were older I took a full time degree in Theology and Philosophy following it with much private study and research into physics, chemistry and cosmology which were relatively new subjects to me. After that I researched some history and archaeology.

There were questions that had no satisfactory answers. This quest helped me to find answers.